A

FAITH **FULL**
marriage

building a lifetime love on biblical principles

paul chappell

All Scripture quotations are taken from
the King James Version.

First published in 2007 by Striving Together Publications, a
ministry of Lancaster Baptist Church, Lancaster, CA 93535.
Striving Together Publications is committed to providing
tried, trusted, and proven books that will further equip local
churches to carry out the Great Commission. Your comments
and suggestions are valued.

Striving Together Publications
4020 E. Lancaster Blvd.
Lancaster, CA 93535
800.201.7748
www.strivingtogether.com

Cover design by Andrew Jones
Layout by Craig Parker
Edited by Cary Schmidt and Danielle Mordh
Assistance by Amanda Michael
Special thanks to our proofreaders.

ISBN 978-1-59894-038-1

Printed in the United States of America

Table of Contents

Introduction

Deep in the heart of every man is a need for companionship—for a helpmeet, a completer who will join him in his journey through life. Even at the dawn of Creation, in a perfect world, God said of Adam, "...It is not good that the man should be alone; I will make him an help meet for him" (Genesis 2:18). Man was created needing help and needing completeness to be found in a lifelong, loving relationship.

In much the same way, God created woman with a desire to be cherished and nurtured in a lifelong relationship. Women also intuitively know, from the innermost part of their hearts, that they have a divine calling to complete others and to help them—to provide nurturing companionship for a lifetime.

This is God's design. It's called marriage. It's a great idea, because it's God's, and in case you're wondering—it still works!

If you haven't noticed, marriage is under attack in the twenty-first century. Some are trying to redefine it, others are trying to abolish it altogether. Recent statistics from various surveys place the national divorce rate in America very close to 50%. Some estimate higher, some lower—but there is no doubt that very close to half of all the people who stand at a wedding altar lovingly exchanging lifetime vows, at some point find themselves in a divorce court exchanging arguments—fighting for the car, the house, the kids, and visitation rights.

In spite of this, there is still a bright future for marriage! And no matter where this book finds you, there is HOPE for *your* marriage! Whether you are preparing for marriage, trying to grow in your marriage, or at your wit's end trying to save your marriage—there is hope for you and your spouse.

Can you identify with the heart-level longing I mentioned a moment ago? Do you sense that longing for a lifetime love? Do you desire a companionship that will span decades with true, passionate, unabating love? Here's a more important question. Are you willing to ask the hard questions and receive the difficult answers? Are you willing to believe in the plan of the Designer? Are you willing to take a close look at God's original plan for life, love, and marriage and follow it?

Our secular entertainment-driven culture has sadly and miserably attempted to redefine love and romance. Unfortunately, most are buying into this new, dumbed down, emotional kind of romance that is as fragile as it is fleeting. The world teaches us that love is like a vapor—a brief emotional sensation that ebbs and flows unpredictably and that must be pursued—chased at all costs—for it might never return.

The problem with this definition of love is that it is not God's—which means it isn't real. It is a myth—a fantasy that never really leads to truth. Chasing this emotion will lead you over a relational cliff every time.

To be sure, God's plan for love and romance involves passion and pleasure—intense emotions of love along the way. It involves many wonderful delights, but these are not the essence. These are not the core of what completes our lives and makes us truly happy.

True love and lifetime companionship are the product of God's design—God's rules and guidelines being followed by faith. Hence, we come to the core message of these pages.

Are you willing to have a *marriage of faith*? Are you willing to know and understand God's instructions, and to follow them by faith, whether they make sense to you or not?

While so many in our culture are following lies, it's time that we return to our Maker. Since marriage is His idea, it's time that we ask Him how it is supposed to work. In some ways, what we will study in these few pages will defy everything you see in culture. It will be a massive paradigm shift away from fantasy land and into the reality of God's promises. Are you willing to take that journey?

You *can* have the marriage for which you've always dreamed, but you must get there God's way. And God's way is always "by faith."

Think of these pages as a guide, leading you through a small, winding path to the depth of intimacy and love that your heart truly craves, but taking you in a direction you didn't expect. At first glance, you may wonder if this path really leads to where you dream of being in your marriage.

At the same time, there is another path, wide and sprawling before you. This path promises to take you to your dream marriage a lot quicker. So many are taking this route, and they seem so happy in the short term! It seems to be working.

But think about it. For most, that path is ending in divorce, or at best, unhappy marriages.

On the path discussed in this book, we're going to journey into "faith." We're going to see the supernatural element of God's blessing—God's touch—upon a relationship. We're going to discover what simple faith—trusting and obeying God—can do in a marriage relationship.

God says in Hebrews 11:6, "But without faith it is impossible to please him: for he that cometh to God must believe that he is, and that he is a rewarder of them that diligently seek him."

Faith is simply trusting God—doing what He says, whether it makes sense or not—just because He said it and just because He's God! In this verse, God says faith is the key to pleasing Him. He promises that He is a rewarder of them that diligently seek Him—those who trust Him and follow His plan tenaciously.

Have these pages come to you as you've reached the "end of your rope" relationally? Are you feeling as though you've tried everything and nothing is working for your marriage? Are you fearful that you will one day be on the wrong side of that 50% divorce statistic? Are you fearful that perhaps that deep, heart longing for a lifetime love will never be a reality in your life?

I have good news. Faith can make the difference in your marriage. Join me on this pathway of paradox and discover that the journey into true love is not at all what you thought it might be. And about the time you're ready to stand back, scratch your head, and say, "You've got to be kidding! God expects me to do that?" Just remember that statistic, and decide to trust God by faith. Decide to go with Him when it doesn't make sense.

God rewards those who go against human reasoning to trust Him. Are you willing to take that kind of risk? Are you willing to swallow your pride in order to discover your spouse? Do you want God's rewards in your marriage?

In the chapters ahead, we will see three major steps of faith you must take to enter into a lifetime companionship. These are the three aspects of marriage in which God says, "jump and trust me to catch you." By way of these pages, I wish to lead you to the spiritual "edge of the cliff"—to the point where God says, "Jump!" I wish to show you biblical principles for marriage that at first will cause you to question and doubt. You will wonder, "Why did God design it this way? Why does God command that?" You will even be tempted to say, "Well, I'm not going to do that!"

Think again about that statistic! Think again about the longing of your heart! Then choose to trust the One who created marriage. Believe that He is a rewarder of them that believe.

Friend, marriage still works, but it only works by faith.

No matter where your marriage is today, faith can make the difference! Let's find out how.

PART ONE

The Faith to Commit

CHAPTER ONE

Faith to Commit

The first stop on our journey brings us to the bedrock foundation of a strong marriage. The word is *commitment*. Few couples even really know what it means, much less how critical it is to the process of building a marriage.

Commitment is a vital ingredient for a strong relationship. You cannot build a long-lasting, joyful marriage without rock-solid commitment from two people.

The problem is that we live in a day where commitment to anything other than self is a thing of the past. The philosophy of the day is, "does it work out for me?" We're committed to anything and everything that furthers *our* pleasure, advances *our* careers, or inflates *our* bank accounts. If it makes us comfortable, we'll commit! We're committed to Visa, Countrywide mortgage, and Ford finance—but we can't find the inner determination or integrity to enter into relational commitment.

The word *commitment* is defined as "devotion or dedication to a cause, person, or relationship." It is also "something that takes up time and energy as an obligation." In God's Word, the word *committed* refers to surrendering or yielding. It implies something so strong that it is literally given over to another and "locked away."

We've lost the significance of this word in our culture. Commitment means this decision is not up for reconsideration. It means that failure is not an option. It means that we're in this relationship together, no matter what—we're not giving up, quitting, or changing course. We're committed! There will be no second guessing. There is no "plan B." We're committed! This will work, or we will die trying—but we're not giving up.

I know what you're thinking. "How can I commit to a relationship that isn't working?" Again, I remind you that this path is a paradox. Commitment is only strong when it goes against the grain—when it is being tested. For this reason it is a matter of faith.

The world says, "Show me and I'll believe." God says, "Believe me, and I'll show you." Even so, many spouses are saying, "Show me a relationship that works, and then I'll commit to it." God says that the formula is the other way around. "Commit to your marriage, and I'll give you a relationship that works."

Are you willing to trust God? Are you willing to have faith in His plan for marriage? Think about that 50% statistic!

A marriage that begins with a "try it and see" proposition is destined to fail. A marriage without commitment is as inoperable as a car without an engine! It might look good coming off the assembly line, but it's not going anywhere! It won't run.

A marriage, from the very foundation, runs on commitment. It is the glue that holds hearts together. It is the fiery determination that forges greatness between two people—great friendship, great love, and a great future.

Commitment in marriage is a vital ingredient for two reasons. First, because God said so. He said of marriage in Genesis 2:24, "Therefore shall a man leave his father and his mother, and shall cleave unto his wife: and they shall be one flesh." The word *cleave* speaks of holding tight with no intention of letting go! Again He says in Matthew 19:6, "Wherefore they are no more twain, but one flesh. What therefore God hath joined together, let not man put asunder."

What God says, works. It's that simple—if you will trust Him.

Second, commitment is vital because it proves love. If you long for a lifetime love, you long for someone to commit to you. You long for someone to overlook your failures, be patient through your faults, and stay with you no matter what. The question is, are you willing to *be* that person as well?

Great marriages didn't always start out great! No one enters into a perfect marriage. No one wakes up every day to a spouse who never lets them down or to a relationship that never experiences trauma.

No, great marriages must be forged! Like a fine vessel from a kiln, they must be hardened and strengthened through the fires of trial and testing. Great love doesn't happen by accident. It is the product of fiery determination not to quit. It is the result of commitment that never questions and never falters.

Friend, if you have an "out"—if you have a "plan B"—then your marriage is destined to fail. The first step of faith that you must take is full, 100%, unflinching commitment. You must determine that nothing will remove you from this relationship. Nothing will cause you to doubt its veracity or potential. No matter how bad circumstances seem or how damaged your relationship feels, commitment says, "I'm staying because I believe that God can rekindle a great, fiery love from the ashes of our injuries!"

Let's take a closer look at this glue that holds great marriages together.

CHAPTER TWO

Committing to Faith in Christ

The kind of commitment that is required for marriage to be all that God intended, begins first with Jesus Christ. Do you know Him personally? Has there been a moment in your life when you placed your full faith in Him to be your personal Saviour? Without Christ in your heart and life, your marriage is destined to mediocrity at best. You might apply these principles, see them work, and actually survive the statistics, but without Christ, you will never know the full love and joy that you could experience.

Each of us enters life with a void in our hearts. The Bible says that we are born in sin—"Behold, I was shapen in iniquity; and in sin did my mother conceive me" (Psalm 51:5). We enter this life separated from God with the price of sin upon our heads. We are condemned already, not because God doesn't love us, but because He cannot allow sin into Heaven. He cannot let sin go unpunished. And since we are all sinners, that makes us "dead to God."

God says in Romans 6:23, "For the wages of sin is death…." This simply means that because of our sin, we are incapable of enjoying a right or close relationship with God personally. Thankfully, the verse continues, "but the gift of God is eternal life through Jesus Christ our Lord."

You see, in His great love, God wasn't willing to simply condemn us to death. He wasn't willing to watch us falter our way through our lives and marriages, and then to condemn us to eternal Hell.

He chose to intervene. He committed Himself to us unconditionally! First Peter 2:21–23 says, "For even hereunto were ye called: because Christ also suffered for us, leaving us an example, that ye should follow his steps: Who did no sin, neither was guile found in his mouth: Who, when he was reviled, reviled not again; when he suffered, he threatened not; but committed himself to him that judgeth righteously."

Christ was so committed to us—He loved us so much that He literally went to the death. "And being found in fashion as a man, he humbled himself, and became obedient unto death, even the death of the cross" (Philippians 2:8).

When Jesus suffered on that cross, He was extending His outstretched arms of commitment to you. He was inviting you into a lifetime relationship with Him—an unconditional loving relationship that rested solely on your faith and His commitment. Thankfully that relationship doesn't rest upon our behavior, our merits, or our goodness. It rests completely on His grace and our willingness to trust Him.

God always makes good on His commitments! He keeps His promises. He never falters and never fails. When you turn to Jesus Christ by faith and invite Him into your heart, it is an irreversible decision. In Hebrews 13:5 He promises, "...I will never leave thee, nor forsake thee."

This is our model in commitment! Jesus' commitment to His Father and to us is a picture of what we are to have toward our spouses.

A personal relationship with Christ and its accompanying love becomes the foundation and standard for the kind of love that makes a great marriage. Without that relationship, not only will you not experience that kind of love from Christ, but you will be incapable of expressing it as well.

In and of ourselves we are incapable of showing the kind of love that Christ gives to us. Yet, when we come to Him in faith and trust Him as our personal Saviour, something marvelous and miraculous occurs.

First, we experience God's committed love personally. For the first time in our lives, the love of Christ floods into our hearts like fresh water on parched soil. We discover that it is *His* great love for which we desperately long.

Second, His Holy Spirit indwells our lives and provides the supernatural change agent that is required to have that same committed love toward our spouses. Ephesians 1:13–14 says, "In whom ye also trusted, after that ye heard the word of truth, the gospel of your salvation: in whom also after that ye believed, ye were sealed with that holy Spirit of promise, Which is the earnest of our inheritance until the redemption of the purchased possession, unto the praise of his glory." We become "able" to be committed the way Christ is. Without His help, we cannot give this kind of committed love, but when He enters our lives, He divinely enables us to do so.

Friend, without Christ, marriage is an empty, disappointing proposition. The committed love that a strong marriage requires is *impossible* apart from Christ. When He is absent from our hearts, the best we can hope for is the ability to simply "get by."

Yet, when Jesus Christ is in our lives and when we are fully committed to Him, marriage becomes the delightful, loving, dedicated adventure that we've always dreamed it would be. The spiritual intimacy that only Christ can give, weaves its way into the fiber of the marriage relationship at a level that nothing can touch.

How could you ever expect to commit to a human relationship if you cannot commit to your Heavenly Father? How could you give selfless, committed love to an imperfect person, if you cannot receive it from a perfect Saviour? How could you ever trust another human being from your heart if you cannot trust your Creator?

If you have never trusted the Lord as your personal Saviour, then I challenge you to do so before you continue reading this book. Take a moment, open your heart, and invite Him into your life to save you from sin's penalty, to forgive you, and to begin His work in you. Take Him at His Word, "For whosoever shall call upon the name of the Lord shall be saved" (Romans 10:13). Pray right now and ask Jesus Christ to save you. Invite Him into your life, your home, and your marriage.

The paradox of faith—in giving your life to Christ, you find a greater life. In giving your marriage to Christ, you discover a greater marriage. In committing to the faith of Christ, you discover the supernatural element that enables you to build a strong marital relationship God's way. If faith in Christ is missing in your heart and marriage, then this is the starting point. This is the birthplace of "A Faith Full Marriage."

Once you know Him as Saviour, His presence in your life changes everything. Suddenly you have a great and loving God who can strengthen you, enlighten you, guide you, and instruct you through any challenge. Suddenly your marital journey itself has a new Companion! When He touches your marriage, it will go to a place you never thought possible.

The Apostle Paul wrote in 2 Timothy 1:12, "...for I know whom I have believed, and am persuaded that he is able to keep that which I have committed unto him against that day."

When you commit your heart and your marriage to Jesus Christ, you're placing it in good hands! He is able to keep it, to grow it, to establish it by His grace.

Commit yourself to Him—to trusting Him—and ask Him to begin helping you build the lifetime love for which you've always dreamed. It all begins with Him. After all—He is the maker of marriage!

CHAPTER THREE

Committing to Total Acceptance

At the age of forty-nine, Bill Zerbe suffered from the early onset of Alzheimer's disease. His wife, Christian author Becky Zerbe, shares that one day, after a troubling season of forgetfulness, he picked up his journal and wrote these words to her:

> *Honey,*
>
> *Today fear is taking over. The day is coming when all my memories of this life we share will be gone. In fact, you and the boys will be gone from me. I will lose you even as I am surrounded by you and your love. I don't want to leave you. I want to*

grow old in the warmth of memories. Forgive me for leaving so slowly and painfully.

Fighting back the tears, she picked up a pen and returned the following message to her husband by way of his journal:

My sweet husband,

What will happen when we get to the point where you no longer know me? I will continue to go on loving you and caring for you—not because you know me or remember our life, but because I remember you. I will remember the man who proposed to me and told me that he loved me, the look on his face when his children were born, the father he was, the way he loved our extended family. I'll recall his love for riding, hiking, and reading; his tears at sentimental movies; the unexpected witty remarks; and how he held my hand when we prayed. I cherish the pleasure, obligation, commitment, and opportunity to care for you because I REMEMBER YOU!"

What a picture of total and complete acceptance!

In Genesis 2:18–25 God recorded the first marriage ceremony—His wonderful work of creating Eve, Adam's helpmeet. Take your time reading it:

"And the LORD God said, It is not good that the man should be alone; I will make him an help meet for him. And out of the ground the LORD God formed every beast of the field, and every fowl of the air; and brought them unto Adam to see what he would call them: and whatsoever Adam called every living creature, that was the name thereof. And Adam gave names to all cattle, and to the fowl of the air, and to every beast of the field; but for Adam there was not found an help meet for him. And the LORD God caused a deep sleep to fall upon Adam, and he slept: and he took one of his ribs, and closed up the flesh instead thereof; And the rib, which the LORD God had taken from man, made he a woman, and brought her unto the man. And Adam said, This is now bone of my bones, and flesh of my flesh: she shall be called Woman, because she was taken out of Man. Therefore shall a man leave his father and his mother, and shall cleave unto his wife: and they shall be one flesh. And they were both naked, the man and his wife, and were not ashamed."

In this beautiful story, we see Adam's immediate and total acceptance of his new bride. He declared, "…this is now bone of my bones, and flesh of my flesh."

His first response to Eve was essentially, "I fully accept you as a part of me!"

The second step in our understanding of commitment is a commitment to total acceptance of your spouse. Once again, Jesus is our model. For He says that we are "to the praise of the glory of his grace, wherein he hath made us accepted in the beloved" (Ephesians 1:6).

Ephesians 5:25 instructs us to mirror Christ's love for the church in our relationships with our wives, "Husbands, love your wives, even as Christ also loved the church, and gave himself for it." Again in verses 28–29 He continues, "So ought men to love their wives as their own bodies. He that loveth his wife loveth himself. For no man ever yet hated his own flesh; but nourisheth and cherisheth it, even as the Lord the church."

The principle of this passage teaches that a great marriage is one in which both spouses give unconditional and total acceptance of the other. In other words, marriage is not a 50/50 proposition, but rather a 100/100 proposition! Marriage only works when there is 100% commitment to each other and 100% acceptance of each other.

When you trusted Christ, He accepted you right where you were, just as you were. He didn't demand change, expect you to earn His love, or command you to do something in return! He simply accepted you—in spite of your faults, your failures, and your sin. Though you had nothing to offer, He freely gave Himself to you. And from the moment of your salvation to the moment you see Him face to face, His love will never have conditions. He fully accepts you as His child.

Does your spouse have this full, unwavering acceptance from you?

Too many marriages today suffer from "conditionitis"—we conduct our relationships as though it is a contract negotiation rather than a loving commitment. We place conditions upon our love. We expect our spouses to change, to perform or to behave a certain way, and when our expectations are not met, our love is not freely given. These conditions keep us from fully accepting each other as God commands.

For the husband, He commands that he "love as Christ loves." For the wife, He commands that she "reverence her husband" (Ephesians 5:25, 33). Both partners in the relationship are commanded to drop their expectations and to fully accept each other.

Committing to full acceptance in your marriage is to say to each other, "As you are today, if you never change, I love you fully, and I will stay with you for life." The foundation of gratitude is the expectation of nothing! And in marriage, full acceptance sets aside expectations and conditions. Full acceptance is the only environment in which unconditional Christlike love can be expressed.

Interestingly, full acceptance is also the optimal environment for change! For within the loving bounds of being totally accepted, we often find a response in kind. In other words, "Since you love me as I am, I strongly desire to love you as you want to be loved! I will be willing to change since that is not what you require!"

It is when our spouses are fully accepted, that they can be free to change by God's grace and purely out of Christlike love!

I warned you that this "Faith Full Marriage" would be a paradox! Have faith in God's plan—accept your spouse unconditionally. Stop setting conditions! Faith works, just wait and see!

CHAPTER FOUR

Committing to Openness and Unity

Someone said, "Being a husband is just like any other job—it's much easier if you like your boss!"

Dwight Eisenhower once said, "Only two things are necessary to keep one's wife happy. The first is to let her think she's having her way. The second is to let her have it."

Believe it or not, getting your way is not the way to build a happy marriage. In fact, it is fighting for "my way" that leads so many couples directly to divorce court.

Our third stop on this study of marital commitment is yet another paradox. We will study it from another angle in a later chapter as well.

In a day when we are taught to look out for "number one," to protect our self-interests, and to hedge our bets, strong marriages take a different path!

Strong marriages are committed to openness and unity. Lifetime romance is discovered as two people let down their guards, drop their defenses, and weave their hearts together in total vulnerability to one another.

God vividly shows us this principle this way, "For this cause shall a man leave his father and mother, and shall be joined unto his wife, and they two shall be one flesh" (Ephesians 5:31).

In this verse, He describes a process that begins at the wedding altar and continues throughout a lifetime. It is a process of opening up to one another and becoming one—one heart, one body, and one spirit. It is a process of leaving, cleaving, and weaving.

In reality, this goes against everything that culture teaches us. Most people would look at this kind of vulnerability as risky and foolish. Most people enter into love relationships and marriage commitments with emotional and relational safeguards in place—a backup plan just in case things don't work out the way they expect. This "plan B" approach prevents a marriage from ever leaving infancy. It withholds the lifeblood of a relationship. This mentality puts a stranglehold on a marriage, cutting off the oxygen supply of intimacy and unity.

For a man and woman to experience the kind of intimate love that Christ desires to give, there must be a "letting down of the guard." There must be vulnerability, transparency, and unity.

For the husband, the command is clear. Leave your father and mother, cleave unto your wife, and be one flesh. For the wife, God's Word is also clear, "Let the husband render unto the wife due benevolence: and likewise also the wife unto the husband" (1 Corinthians 7:3). We are both commanded to "render" to one another "due benevolence." In other words, we are commanded to fully give our hearts, our spirits, and our bodies to one another in total unity and openness for the strength of the relationship.

Your marriage relationship is three dimensional, much like your person. As you are made up of body, soul, and spirit, even so your marriage has a spiritual dimension (faith in Christ), an emotional dimension (your expressed love and faith in each other), and a physical dimension (your physical love relationship and the joining of your bodies into "one flesh").

For many, if not most marriages, the spiritual dimension is completely ignored, while the emotional dimension is neglected or poorly maintained. Understandably, both of these dimensions then negatively impact the physical dimension of marriage leaving us feeling "unhappily married" at best.

The unmet needs of our spirits, our hearts, and our bodies leave us wallowing in desperation and vulnerable to despair and hopelessness. This creates a downward spiral of discouragement and temptation— to quit, to leave, or to find love somewhere else!

Ironically, in these scenarios, love is not gone or dead between us. It is merely neglected. Like a fire where no wood has been added—the flames are dying. Rather than find another firepit or gather around someone else's fire, we simply need to put more fuel on the relationship. We need to renew our commitment to openness and unity.

Friend, let me share a mental picture. Imagine two fists tightly balled up next to each other. Those fists picture many marriages. Two hearts, tightly closed— clenched in anger, resentment, disappointment, or bitterness toward one another. For those fists to unite into "one flesh" they must first open. The clenching must release, the fingers must uncurl, and the hand must open.

Now picture two hands wide open with fingers spread. Gradually move those hands together, palm against palm. As the hands clasp, the fingers interlock and the two hands become one unit, tightly cleaving and weaving together.

This is a picture of what a biblical marriage should be. Hard hearts must open. Disappointed souls must soften. The cold spirit must "unclench" and open up to the possibility of unity. Then the two must come together, each giving to the other so that the two can become one.

There is a reason that this particular commitment is our third stop. Faith in Christ is the decision of a moment. Total acceptance is as well. But openness and unity is the process of a lifetime! This is something you will have to commit to over the long term. It will not happen immediately. It isn't created overnight. But it can happen if you will give yourself to Christ and to His process of making your lives one.

This act of leaving, cleaving, and weaving is not something that you conquer. It's not a task that you check off your list to move on to another. This is a day by day, month by month, year by year process of growing.

It requires commitment for the simple fact that it takes *time*. Some days you will sense the fruit of success while other days you will feel distant and defeated. But over time—over decades—your commitment to building unity through openness will be evident. Your heart will reap the benefits.

Several things can immediately kill the spiritual openness and unity in a marriage. Selfishness or a desire to control can cause us to close. Insecurity or a lack of feeling "safe" can cause us to withhold our hearts. And competition can cause us to resent or envy our spouses.

Yet several actions encourage openness and unity as well. Unconditional acceptance opens the heart. Encouraging, tender words and expressions of gratitude soften the spirit. Gentleness and selflessness always go farther toward openness with a spouse than anything else. Billy Sunday once said, "Try praising your wife even if it does scare her at first!"

You really have two choices. You can harden your heart and withhold what your spouse desperately needs regarding openness and unity, or you can risk everything, trust God in faith, and give in. Soften your heart.

When you look at your marriage relationship, do you see a closed clenched fist, or an open palm? Is the spirit of your marriage hard or soft? Are your hearts turned toward each other, longing for unity, or turned against each other mulling in resentment?

If you want that great marriage God promises, you must commit yourself to unity through openness. You must unclench your spirit and move toward your spouse. Soften your heart toward your lifetime companion! Don't wait for your spouse to make the first move. Be the first one to loosen the stranglehold and see how God will bless your faith.

Commitment is the missing first ingredient in most marriages today. We've seen commitment to Christ, commitment to total acceptance, and commitment to unity through openness.

Sadly, we live in an age of quitters. We live in a day when even many Christians walk around with the "last straw" in their front pocket. We're too quick to use the word "divorce." We're too quick to question and second guess our decisions to marry. We whip out that "last straw" on a whim!

What is commitment in marriage? Commitment simply means that you don't even have a "last straw."

Do you have the faith to fully commit? Do you have a dogged defiance toward quitting? Without this ingredient, nothing else will matter.

Someone once said, "A man who wants something will find a way. A man who doesn't will find an excuse." Decide now to take the first step to a strong marriage: Commitment by faith.

PART TWO

The Faith to Yield

CHAPTER FIVE

Abandoning Our Willful Spirits

Two neighbors were talking over their backyard fence one day. "I went to a wedding this weekend," said one, "but I don't think the marriage will last."

"Why not?" asked the other.

"Well, when the groom said, 'I do,' the bride said, 'don't use that tone of voice with me!'"

One of the greatest obstacles to building a strong marriage is our strong wills! When left to itself, stubborn self-will enlarges itself and dominates our lives and marriages. Many marriages, over time, are reduced to nothing more than a battle for control—a battle for "my own way."

In this section, we will study yet another paradox—another faith step that is required in a great marriage. Perhaps more than any other part of this book, your flesh will fight this principle. You won't naturally want to do this, but the results will be well worth the sacrifice!

In every great marriage—every "Faith Full Marriage"—there is an enduring commitment to *yielding* to one another. To yield means to present yourself in service to another. It literally means that you must become the servant of your spouse. I know it doesn't make human sense, but it is a biblical principle that God always blesses. We must learn to trust Him in faith.

Have you ever noticed how we all enter life rather self-centered? Just take a trip to your church nursery some time. You'll see relatively young children fighting for toys, screaming for their own way, and generally acting out the natural tendency of the flesh to bow to the will of self.

Throughout our lives, it is natural (not spiritual) for all of us to think of ourselves first. In reality, if you were to think back to the time when you were dating your spouse and even in your early marriage, you were probably more self-driven than others-focused. You liked this person. He was attractive to you. She was beautiful. You liked the way this person made you feel.

Often in pre-marital counseling I hear couples explain what attracted them to each other, and it's almost always self-centered. They say things such as, "This person has all the qualities I've ever wanted in a spouse." "He makes me feel like no one else can." "She treats me with the kind of love I've always dreamed of having."

Early in our relationships, our natural tendency is to live for self. Hence, each of us comes into marriage with a large sense of "what I want!" You might call them unspoken expectations—some that we don't even realize we have until they aren't met!

These selfish expectations form our wills, and their strength and stubbornness is seen the first time we are disappointed. The first time our spouse "lets us down" our stubborn will rears its head, quenches our spirits toward each other, and fights for its own way.

Before long, many marriages become more like a tug-of-war contest than a honeymoon! The relationship becomes a literal standoff. Two stubborn people holding out on each other until the other surrenders. In the midst of this process, our wills entrench themselves, refusing to yield, refusing to let go. Then, out of hurt and resentment, the situation accelerates. Our words become cutting; our attitudes unyielding; and our hearts toward each other become cold and unrelenting.

All of this hurt simply because "I didn't get my way." Sad, isn't it? It's sad that we would so allow the dreams of our hearts to die on the altar of selfishness. It's sad that our behavior in marriage so often resembles the children in the church nursery.

The Bible predicted this kind of behavior in 2 Timothy 3:1–5, "This know also, that in the last days perilous times shall come. For men shall be lovers of their own selves, covetous, boasters, proud, blasphemers, disobedient to parents, unthankful, unholy, Without natural affection, trucebreakers, false accusers, incontinent, fierce, despisers of those that are good, Traitors, heady, highminded, lovers of pleasures more than lovers of God; Having a form of godliness, but denying the power thereof: from such turn away."

Think about that—"men shall be lovers of their own selves" and that self-love will drive them to destructive behavior in precious relationships.

As in part one, we discovered that the primary flaw of marriages in the twenty-first century is "faithlessness." We might say that the second great destroyer of marriages is "selfishness."

Friend, focusing on "your needs" will ruin your marriage! God says the key to marital bliss is discovered in "giving in." It is found in yielding.

This paradox will drive you nuts if you try to explain or reason it. It doesn't make sense in our flesh, but through the eyes of faith, it works. In marriage, you win by losing. You get by giving. You live by dying to self.

I believe that there are three basic areas in which we must learn to yield—to give in—if we will experience great marriages! Continue reading to discover more of what God's Word teaches regarding a yielded spirit.

CHAPTER SIX

Yielding to the Scriptures

The Bible is God's Word to men—His instruction book for life—and throughout His Word, God teaches us to surrender. While this goes against our grain, it is the secret to experiencing God's best in our lives. Do you want God's best in your marriage? Do you desire God's blessing upon your relationship? Then you must discover this principle of death to self and submission to God and others.

In Romans 6:13, God instructs us to yield our bodies to Him, "Neither yield ye your members as instruments of unrighteousness unto sin: but yield yourselves unto God, as those that are alive from the dead, and your members as instruments of righteousness unto God."

In Romans 12:1 we see, "I beseech you therefore, brethren, by the mercies of God, that ye present your bodies a living sacrifice, holy, acceptable unto God, which is your reasonable service."

Again in James 4:7 we are taught, "Submit yourselves therefore to God. Resist the devil, and he will flee from you."

This act of surrender is pivotal in every area of the Christian life. Learning to give in to God and to submit ourselves to His laws, His commands, and His guidelines is critical to having His joy in our hearts.

Jesus is our first and greatest picture of submission. He first exemplified it by humbling Himself to become a man and to take our death upon the cross. He often referred to Himself as the "son of man." Think about the Creator of all the universe stooping to call Himself the son of His creation! It was Jesus who washed the disciples feet, who spent His earthly life serving society's outcasts.

Jesus taught this principle as well. He said, "But it shall not be so among you: but whosoever will be great among you, let him be your minister" (Matthew 20:26). He said, "For the Son of man is come to seek and to save that which was lost" (Luke 19:10). He constantly lived in subjection to the will of His Heavenly Father— "For I came down from heaven, not to do mine own will, but the will of him that sent me" (John 6:38).

The Bible is very strong on this point. We are commanded over and over again to let our selfish wills die and to surrender our lives to God. We are commanded to live in subjection—to let God's will rule and guide our lives. We are commanded to lay down our arms and quit fighting.

It is very critical that you first understand, when you fight your spouse—your will against his or hers— you are actually fighting God. The highest principle of submission is that we are to first submit our lives to God and to His Word.

Our battle of wills in marriage is merely evidence of a much deeper battle of wills with God! And the first step to ending these battles of will is to surrender our wills to God. The first point of yielding must be to God and His Word.

Friend, you may be doing a lot of good things in your life. You may be attending church, giving offerings, being nice to your neighbors, and working hard on the job—but none of these good deeds is a replacement for basic Bible application. None of these give you the right to resist God's authority in your life.

So, who is the final authority in your life? By what standard do you make your decisions? By what principles do you choose your course? Is it by your own will—your own selfish whim? Or are you fully and completely surrendered to seeking and obeying the will of God as expressed in His Word?

God's Word must be your final authority in all matters. You must have this foundation or else your marriage has no solid ground. You cannot afford to rest your marriage on your selfish whim or personal agenda. This is shifting sand, but God's Word is a rock!

For your marriage to truly mature and be all that it can be, you must fully yield to God and His Word. You must say, "God, I give in. I will not knowingly resist what you have said. I will seek to know your Word, apply it to my life, and obey it daily. God, I crown you as my final authority. You are my God, and my selfish will bows to your Word."

Take a moment and consider what these passages teach us about the place of God's Word in our lives.

"Now ye are clean through the word which I have spoken unto you."—John 15:3

"Sanctify them through thy truth: thy word is truth."—John 17:17

"And ye shall know the truth, and the truth shall make you free."—John 8:32

"For this cause also thank we God without ceasing, because, when ye received the word of God which ye heard of us, ye received it not as the word of men, but as it is in truth, the word of God, which effectually worketh also in you that believe."—1 Thessalonians 2:13

"For the word of God is quick, and powerful, and sharper than any twoedged sword, piercing even to the dividing asunder of soul and spirit, and of the joints and marrow, and is a discerner of the thoughts and intents of the heart."—Hebrews 4:12

"I have written unto you, fathers, because ye have known him that is from the beginning. I have written unto you, young men, because ye are strong, and the word of God abideth in you, and ye have overcome the wicked one."—1 John 2:14

Will you make a paradigm shift in your life? Will you lay down your will and take up God's? Will you yield to Him? Will you make His Word your final authority—the foundation for your life's direction? If so, the next two steps will be much easier!

You're well on your way to discovering the magnificent power of "yielding"!

CHAPTER SEVEN

Yielding to the Holy Spirit

When you really consider the monumental task of maintaining a good marriage, it can be overwhelming! How can two imperfect, selfish human beings weave their lives together to become one? If it seems that this task is too big for you, too hard to even comprehend, and too much to ask, then you are correct!

A great marriage requires more wisdom, more spiritual insight, and more power than we have in ourselves. It is far beyond our human strength and abilities.

Thankfully, this is where faith comes back into the picture! God has not left us alone in this responsibility; He actually offers to "get involved." He stipulates that His power and His guidance are prerequisites for success in our marriages, in our lives, and in our homes.

He says in Ephesians 5:18–20, "And be not drunk with wine, wherein is excess; but be filled with the Spirit; Speaking to yourselves in psalms and hymns and spiritual songs, singing and making melody in your heart to the Lord; Giving thanks always for all things unto God and the Father in the name of our Lord Jesus Christ."

While the world is yielding to alcohol, drugs, pleasure, hedonism, and other forms of emotional painkillers, God offers a completely different solution to life. He says, "be filled with the Spirit." The word *filled* means to make full, to render full, or to complete. The implication is, without this filling, we are hopelessly insufficient for the task set before us.

When left to ourselves, we are most often led by emotions, by issues of the heart, by culture, or by self-will. Each of these will take your life and marriage in the wrong direction—every time.

What we desperately need is a different guide! We need God's personal and powerful presence every moment of every day—guiding our hearts, filtering our words, bringing our thoughts and actions into line with His desires. We need God's power to supernaturally enable us to develop the marriage relationship for which we've always dreamed.

If you are feeling that this task is beyond you—good! It is. But it isn't beyond God, and He offers you His power and presence right now.

While yielding to the Scripture (as we learned in the last chapter) is a broader decision, yielding to the Holy Spirit is a moment by moment, daily choice. It is something that you must return to again and again.

The moment you trusted Christ, God took up residence in your life. He came to live within you. From that moment until now, His Holy Spirit has desired to guide you, teach you, comfort you, convict you, change you, and enable you in every area of your life. He is the very presence of God in your spirit, and He is desiring to change you from the inside out.

This is not some spooky or emotional experience. It's not some wild religious sensation. It is the simple fact that God lives within you and desires to lead and guide you. It means you have divine help in building your marriage—if you will yield to it!

Every day, moment by moment, you have a decision to make. Will you yield to the Holy Spirit? Will you seek His filling and guidance? Or will you ignore His presence only to be directed by your own will and emotions. God says in 1 Thessalonians 5:19, "Quench not the Spirit." In Ephesians 4:30 He says, "And grieve not the holy Spirit of God, whereby ye are sealed unto the day of redemption."

You see, each day we either seek and ask for the filling of the Holy Spirit, or we deny His presence and let our self-will take control.

How do we yield to this wonderful presence of God within us? (Once again, faith comes into the picture!) You acknowledge His presence and you make a choice—"Holy Spirit, I acknowledge you in my life today. I surrender my will and ask you to fill me. I desire to hear your guidance and to follow your promptings. I desire to obey your impulses. Please fill me, overcome my will with yours, and change my heart today."

This should be a day by day and even a moment by moment decision. No single prayer could make a greater difference in the daily growth and maturity of your marriage than this! No fight can withstand this kind of spiritual yielding. No stubbornness can maintain its stronghold after such a prayer. The spiritual battle for your marriage will be won as you daily ask the Holy Spirit to fill and control you.

By the way, when you pray this prayer, you certainly won't feel any different! Don't expect feelings. Just trust in faith that God will hear your prayer and work in your heart in subtle ways. He will lead you, prompt you, and guide you step by step.

You cannot yield to the Holy Spirit without being changed. Chances are your spouse will see it sooner than you do, but rest assured—true spiritual, inner change happens first by the power of God's Holy Spirit.

No home or church can succeed without the fullness of the Spirit in a person's life. The secret of harmony in the home is the fullness of the Spirit. The unity of the church and of the home both depend on the Spirit. It is God's power from within, not pressure and guilt from without, that holds the home together.

When you yield to the Holy Spirit, He will change your life, your attitude, and your perspective. He will give you inner joy coupled with outward thankfulness. He will settle and establish your heart, give you renewed strength and desire, and enable you to love selflessly.

Once you get to know the Holy Spirit—once you establish a habit of yielding to Him daily—you will recognize deep and lasting change in your heart and home. You and your marriage will be delightfully different. Pray with the psalmist, "Cast me not away from thy presence; and take not thy holy spirit from me" (Psalm 51:11).

Friend, if you will yield to the Scriptures as the final authority of your life and yield to the Holy Spirit as your daily guide and strength, then the third area of yielding will be a "piece of cake"!

CHAPTER EIGHT

Yielding to Your Spouse

After bringing their first baby home from the hospital, one wife suggested to her husband that he try his hand at changing diapers. "I'm busy," he said. "I'll do the next one."

Sometime later, noticing that the baby was wet, she asked if he was ready to learn how to change diapers. He gave her a puzzled look, then with a realizing chuckle he finally said, "Oh, Honey, when I said 'I'll do the next one' I didn't mean the next diaper. I meant the next baby!"

Why is it that we struggle with giving in to the will of another—especially our spouses?

This is where yielding becomes intensely practical and personal! This is where our battle of wills has its most intense struggle—against another person. Yielding to the Scripture and to the Spirit is one thing, but yielding to the person I'm trying to win against? Now that's another thing altogether!

For many reasons, the very idea of yielding to our spouses often meets immediate resistance in the heart. Our pride and our flesh rear up in defiance as if to say, "But my spouse doesn't deserve this kind of treatment!" True—none of us do. But that's not the principle.

God teaches that husbands and wives are to selflessly yield to each other—preferring each other, giving to each other, and serving each other—unconditionally and unreservedly! This concept is foreign in our culture, and once again requires faith!

The church today has been engulfed in, identified with, and victimized by worldly philosophies and standards. Consequently, many of the concepts of God's Word are offensive to the modern Christian. Even the thought of submitting or yielding to our spouses is offensive.

Look carefully at the beautiful picture of the marriage relationship in this passage and notice how the relationship is to be characterized by mutual submission—each preferring the other before self:

"Submitting yourselves one to another in the fear of God. Wives, submit yourselves unto your own husbands, as unto the Lord. For the husband is the head of the wife, even as Christ is the head of the church: and he is the saviour of the body. Therefore as the church is subject unto Christ, so let the wives be to their own husbands in every thing. Husbands, love your wives, even as Christ also loved the church, and gave himself for it; That he might sanctify and cleanse it with the washing of water by the word, That he might present it to himself a glorious church, not having spot, or wrinkle, or any such thing; but that it should be holy and without blemish. So ought men to love their wives as their own bodies. He that loveth his wife loveth himself. For no man ever yet hated his own flesh; but nourisheth and cherisheth it, even as the Lord the church: For we are members of his body, of his flesh, and of his bones. For this cause shall a man leave his father and mother, and shall be joined unto his wife, and they two shall be one flesh. This is a great mystery: but I speak concerning Christ and the church. Nevertheless let every one of you in particular so love his wife even as himself;

and the wife see that she reverence her husband."
—EPHESIANS 5:21–31

In this passage, both spouses are first commanded to submit to each other. Then, husbands are commanded to love as Christ loves, to nurture, to cherish, to protect, and to cleave unto his wife. Wives are commanded to submit to their husbands. This is a two-way submission—each giving to the other what they desperately need and long for, but each doing so irrespective of the behavior of the other! This is not an "if you then I" proposition! Christ didn't say, "If you will love me, then I will save you!" There are to be no conditions or negotiations in this yielding. It is to be 100% voluntary and independent of the actions of another.

Simply put, if you wait until your spouse "deserves" this submission (in your eyes), you will always be able to find fault or failure. You will always rationalize why your spouse doesn't deserve this kind of selfless love. But viewed through the eyes of Scripture and through the love of Christ, this submission can be freely given "as unto the Lord" (v. 22).

Mutual submission is the key to a winning marital relationship! Mutual submission is when both spouses fully commit to meeting the needs of the other for the glory of God. Mutual submission is when your goal in life becomes two-fold—to please Jesus Christ and to please your spouse!

To put it bluntly, where there is a matter of preference (not matters of faith or biblical principle) you are commanded to yield to your spouse's desires. Where you *can* give in, you *should*.

Do you argue over what restaurants to visit, what music to listen to, and what amount to spend on Christmas gifts? Do you debate over matters of personal preference? Are there areas where you are facing a standoff for no other reason than self-will?

What does God say? Give in. Give your spouse what he or she desires. Yield. Submit. Give honor and preference to one another, just as Jesus did!

Philippians 2:1–5 gives us this picture, "If there be therefore any consolation in Christ, if any comfort of love, if any fellowship of the Spirit, if any bowels and mercies, Fulfil ye my joy, that ye be likeminded, having the same love, being of one accord, of one mind. Let nothing be done through strife or vainglory; but in lowliness of mind let each esteem other better than themselves. Look not every man on his own things, but every man also on the things of others. Let this mind be in you, which was also in Christ Jesus."

Joyce Rogers, the wife of the late Dr. Adrian Rogers wrote, "To prove submission is a wonderful concept, Jesus became the ultimate illustration of its validity. Although He was coequal and coeternal with the Father, He was completely submissive to the Father's will."

In the same way, we are commanded to submit ourselves to each other. In Ephesians 5, both spouses are first commanded to yield to each other, and then in verse 22, the wife is commanded to voluntarily submit to the authority of her husband and to be in subjection to his headship in the home. This in no way implies that the wife is of lesser value or significance. It merely shows God's order of accountability and authority when it comes to the home. As Christ is the head of the church, so the husband should be the head of the home.

When husbands learn to prefer their wives and wives learn to submit to their husbands, they discover a joy that only faith can create! When we trust God's plan and simply obey Him from the heart, marriage becomes what He designed it to be—a lifetime, loving relationship in which two people are abundantly blessed by each other!

We see this principle again in 1 Peter, "Likewise, ye younger, submit yourselves unto the elder. Yea, all of you be subject one to another, and be clothed with humility: for God resisteth the proud, and giveth grace to the humble" (1 Peter 5:5). And Romans 12:10 states, "Be kindly affectioned one to another with brotherly love; in honour preferring one another."

The day you discover the blessedness of yieldedness, your marriage will take a wonderful turn for the better, and Christlike love will take center stage in your relationship.

Starting today, let your life be characterized by selfless living for your spouse. Learn to give, serve, and please your lifetime companion. Lay down your will and give in to your spouse's.

Let's take a look at some practical ways that husbands and wives can yield to each other on a daily basis:

Ten Needs of a Wife
She needs confidence that flows from your spiritual leadership.
She needs assurance that she is meeting your needs.
She needs joy in knowing that you delight in her as a person.

She needs peace in knowing you understand her limitations.
She needs the comfort of knowing that you lovingly protect her.
She needs your focused attention and quality conversation.
She needs to know you are committed to her above everything else.
She needs to trust that you will not willingly deceive her.
She needs loving affection that doesn't lead to the bedroom.
She needs your Christlike leadership and spiritual headship.

Ten Needs of a Husband

He needs to be respected for who he is and what he does.
He needs to be physically intimate with you frequently.
He needs your gratitude for how hard he works to care for you.
He needs your companionship in recreational activities.
He needs your admiration and verbal encouragement.
He needs a warm and welcoming home environment.
He needs a home that is well kept and orderly.
He needs you to give attention to being physically attractive.
He needs you to learn how to make his favorite foods his way.
He needs you to stand behind him cheering him on in life.

Friend, we've seen three types of yielding that must happen for your marriage to truly be "great"! First, you must yield to God and His Word as your final authority. Second, you must daily yield to the Holy Spirit of God to guide you, transform you, and empower you to love as Christ loves. Third, you must daily yield to the pleasures and will of your spouse.

Giving in can be a tough battle. Self-will is strong, and sometimes it dies a slow, miserable death. But the day your will dies, is the day that a new level of love is born in your marriage.

Yielding—mutual submission has great rewards. It is an act of faith that God blesses. And besides all this, an exhaustive study has shown that no woman has ever shot her husband while he was doing the dishes!

PART THREE

3

The Faith to Renew

CHAPTER NINE

Renewing Your Marriage Spiritually

As we take the final step on this journey of faith, there is one more paradox to study in your marriage relationship.

Our world believes that love maintains itself. Culture seems to teach that love is an emotion that is self-sustaining and self-propagating—independently growing apart from any external factors or choices. Following closely behind this lie is another—the lie that relationships are static—that once they are strong, they are always strong and they don't need to be cared for in the same way that a car or a house needs to be cared for.

These two deceptions lead to devastating misunderstandings about the nature of the marriage relationship. These two false beliefs cause us to stop caring for love—to stop fueling it and feeding it. They cause us to treat our marriages like something to be conquered and achieved rather than a relational process that experiences change and growth.

Let's dispel the first lie—love is *not* self-maintaining. Spiritual, Christlike love is a choice—a decision that can be made and remade. It can be renewed and re-decided frequently. Relational love—that romantic feeling between two people—is an emotion that can be fueled or quenched. Like a fire requires maintenance, fuel, fresh wood, and stirring—even so, marital love and the feelings of romance between you and your spouse will ebb and flow. Circumstances, pressure, life-trials, financial burden, health concerns, and a thousand other external factors can threaten to rain on that fire!

Wise couples understand that the flame of love must be fueled regularly. It must be *renewed* and strengthened on a daily and weekly basis so the flame remains strong. God's Word compares love to a flame in Song of Solomon 8:6–7, "Set me as a seal upon thine heart, as a seal upon thine arm: for love is strong as death; jealousy is cruel as the grave: the coals thereof are coals of fire, which hath a most vehement flame. Many waters cannot quench love, neither can the floods drown it: if a man would give all the substance of his house for love, it would utterly be contemned."

"Many waters cannot quench love"—that's a strong love, a raging flame! But this kind of fiery love doesn't happen by accident. It is the product of intent.

Let's dispel the second lie for a moment—relationships are not static. Once relationships are strong, they do not necessarily stay that way. They are dynamic—constantly in a state of change and development. Your relationships are always in motion. They are always headed in some direction. They are always either getting *stronger* or *weaker.*

This lie causes us to disengage once we feel we've reached a point of strength. We fall prey to the thinking that in a relationship success is a "destination." Once we believe we have "arrived," we will stop pursuing and developing deeper love.

Our relationships are not static. They can improve or decline rapidly, depending upon how we fuel and develop them!

Once you have climbed the mountain of *commitment* and scaled the peaks of *yieldedness,* this is your next mountain range—*renewal*. Your relationship will not stay strong unless you understand the built-in dynamic of *renewal*.

Just as your lungs constantly need fresh oxygen, your body constantly needs fresh water and balanced meals, and your fireplace needs fresh wood (or natural gas)—even so, your life and marriage needs regular renewal on several levels. Your marital love will not maintain itself, and it will not remain the same. Keeping love alive is no more difficult than keeping a fire burning—it doesn't take rocket science, just fresh fuel! Keeping love burning brightly is a paradigm shift that causes you to evaluate and renew that love on a weekly and even a daily basis.

Your marriage relationship needs consistent attention. The bad news is, to the extent that you believe the two lies mentioned earlier, your heart will disengage and your love will grow distant and cold. The good news is, no matter where your love is currently, it's not hard to rekindle the flames. Starting a fire is easy. Restarting a fire is just as easy. No, you don't need to go find fire somewhere else. You don't need another spouse, another location, or another fantasy. You simply need to reengage—and to understand the principles of renewal that God shows us in His Word.

First, let's discover spiritual renewal. This ties in closely with our study of yielding to the Holy Spirit. God teaches us that He wants to change us from the inside out. He wants to make us new—to remove the old qualities of our characters and to replace them with Christlike qualities.

Look at what God says in Ephesians 4:22–32:

> *"That ye put off concerning the former conversation the old man, which is corrupt according to the deceitful lusts; And be renewed in the spirit of your mind; And that ye put on the new man, which after God is created in righteousness and true holiness. Wherefore putting away lying, speak every man truth with his neighbour: for we are members one of another. Be ye angry, and sin not: let not the sun go down upon your wrath: Neither give place to the devil. Let him that stole steal no more: but rather let him labour, working with his hands the thing which is good, that he may have to give to him that needeth. Let no corrupt communication proceed out of your mouth, but that which is good to the use of edifying, that it may minister grace unto the hearers. And grieve not the holy Spirit of God, whereby ye are sealed unto the day of redemption. Let all bitterness, and wrath, and anger, and clamour, and evil speaking, be put away from you, with all malice:*

And be ye kind one to another, tenderhearted, forgiving one another, even as God for Christ's sake hath forgiven you."

Do you see the contrast? God desires to renew us spiritually—to take away the old qualities and to replace them with new qualities! He desires to take away anger, bitterness, lying, corrupt communication and to replace those characteristics with kindness, tenderheartedness, and forgiveness.

This is more than turning over a new leaf or merely chipping off some rough edges. This is a renewal of your inner life—a complete remodeling of your heart.

Your spiritual life, like any relationship, is dynamic. It's headed somewhere. It's changing, even now. And in God's design, it should always be in a state of renewal! You should always be growing in grace and becoming more like Christ. Your spiritual life should always be headed in the right direction—shedding more and more of the old nature and taking on more and more of Christ's nature.

This renewing process is vital for your marriage relationship, but it is intensely personal! You cannot mandate this in your spouse's heart. You can only commit and yield yourself to God's process of renewal in your own heart. As you personally become more and more like the new nature of Christ, your love for each other will continue to grow stronger and brighter with each passing day. In other words, when two people are being spiritually renewed in their marriage, they can look forward to a stronger more enjoyable love for decades to come! This kind of love doesn't grow stale—ever! It grows brighter and better, because the Holy Spirit of God is renewing both partners for life!

What a great promise and wonderful hope! What a great process that God offers to carry out in our lives. The choice is yours. Will you allow God to renew you? Will you daily spend time with Him, letting Him change your heart? Will you seek His help in "putting off the old and putting on the new"?

God says in 2 Corinthians 5:17, "Therefore if any man be in Christ, he is a new creature: old things are passed away; behold, all things are become new."

Spiritual renewal is a vital process to a growing marriage. As both partners yield to God's transforming work, they become more like Christ together—and marriage becomes more enjoyable and more loving!

In today's culture, many couples are sharing a roof but not a life—and even many Christian couples are sharing a life, but not a Spirit-filled life! Many today are more comfortable at Starbucks than they are at home.

This shouldn't be the reality of our marriages. Relationships are not static and love does not maintain itself. For this reason, you and your spouse need constant, daily spiritual renewal. You need a vibrant personal walk with Christ that breathes fresh spiritual oxygen into your heart every morning.

Go to God; get alone with Him; and let His process of spiritual renewal find its way into your life and marriage! You will never be the same.

CHAPTER TEN

Renewing Your Marriage Relationally

What percentage of married people actually married someone who turned out to be completely different than they thought they would be?

The answer?—100%.

This isn't bad news—it's just reality. The longer you stay together and the deeper you grow in love, the more you discover the person you married. God designed marriage to be a lifelong pursuit of the heart of another! He never intends for your relationship to be on auto-pilot or to be set to "cruise control"! He expects you to fully engage—all of your heart—for

Him and for your home. He expects you to commit, to yield, and to constantly renew.

In the last chapter we learned about spiritual renewal—the work of the Holy Spirit in your heart personally. Now, you must learn to apply this renewal principle to your daily marriage relationship.

I challenge you to give yourself to fueling the fire of love practically and frequently in your marriage. Put fresh wood on the fire daily. Breathe fresh air into your marriage throughout the day. Discover what fuels your spouse's heart and give him or her that fuel as much as you possibly can.

I believe there are several practical and powerful "fuels" that we can use every day in our marriages to keep love renewed on a daily basis. Let's look at them:

The Fuel of Forgiveness

Johnny and Bobby were good friends who got into a quarrel. In frustration, they went their separate ways, but the next morning Johnny took his cap and headed for Bobby's house once again.

Surprised, an older member of the family said teasingly, "What? Going to play with Bobby again? I thought you quarreled last night and were never going to be friends again."

Johnny looked a little sheepish, dug his toe into the carpet for a moment, then flashed a satisfied smile as he hurried away. "Aww! Bobby and me's good forgetters!"

Great marriages are made up of great forgivers—great forgetters! Disappointment is inevitable in your marriage relationship. The reality is, we are human and we let each other down. Sometimes it's unintentional, while other times it is born out of stubborn will and self-centeredness. The longer you stay together, the more you must discover the awesome power of forgiveness.

Weak marriages are made up of scorekeepers. Strong marriages are made up of grace givers.

Perhaps one of the greatest biblical illustrations of forgiveness is Joseph. Joseph went from being a favored son, to a slave, to a faithful steward, to a forgotten prisoner, to the second in command in Egypt. Years after his brothers sold him into slavery, he said in Genesis 50:20, "But as for you, ye thought evil against me; but God meant it unto good, to bring to pass, as it is this day, to save much people alive."

Forgiveness in marriage is recognizing that God uses even the failures and flaws of your spouse to challenge you and to grow you in faith. In this kind of marriage relationship, even imperfections become allies as God's sovereignty builds you and strengthens you, even through your struggles.

First Peter 3:7–8 says, "Likewise, ye husbands, dwell with them according to knowledge, giving honour unto the wife, as unto the weaker vessel, and as being heirs together of the grace of life; that your prayers be not hindered. Finally, be ye all of one mind, having compassion one of another, love as brethren, be pitiful, be courteous."

Colossians 3:13 says, "Forbearing one another, and forgiving one another, if any man have a quarrel against any: even as Christ forgave you, so also do ye." And Ephesians 4:32 teaches, "And be ye kind one to another, tenderhearted, forgiving one another, even as God for Christ's sake hath forgiven you."

Forgiveness is a wonderful fuel for renewing your marriage relationship. Become a good forgetter and put this fuel on your fire every day.

The Fuel of Reconciliation

Someone once said, "It is more rewarding to resolve a conflict than to dissolve a relationship." The pursuit of resolution says to your spouse, "I love you so much that I will stay here until this problem is taken care of!" Rather than the silent treatment or some other manipulative behavior, mature marriages work things out. They talk, they pray, and they refuse to let something go unresolved.

Conflict in marriage is inevitable. You will never eradicate it completely from your home, but you can deal with it biblically and with spiritual maturity.

Allow me to share with you ten "wrong ways" to handle marital conflict.

Ten Wrong Ways to Handle Conflict
1. *Denying that a problem even exists*
2. *The silent treatment (relational withdrawal)*
3. *Emotional outbursts (adult temper tantrums)*
4. *Walking away and refusing to work it out*
5. *Verbal sparring with hurtful words (trying to win an argument rather than resolve the problem)*
6. *Bringing up past failures (viewing today's conflict through yesterday's pain)*
7. *Shifting the blame and not admitting my own failure*
8. *Ignoring the problem and pretending it will go away*
9. *Failing to seek the Holy Spirit's guidance through prayer*
10. *Refusing to say, "I was wrong; I'm sorry; will you forgive me?"*

Be careful about wrongly responding to conflict. Decide to fuel your love by resolving every problem as quickly as you can.

The Fuel of Encouraging Words

Frustrated at always being corrected by her husband, one woman decided that the next time she would have a comeback. When the moment arrived, she said, "You know, even a broken clock is right *once* a day." Her husband looked at her and flatly replied, "Twice."

Isn't that sometimes how our marriage relationship goes? We seem to miss all the good and positive things about our spouses, while the smallest of failures jumps out loudly at us!

Look at what God says about the power of positive words:

> *"Let no corrupt communication proceed out of your mouth, but that which is good to the use of edifying, that it may minister grace unto the hearers."*
> —EPHESIANS 4:29

> *"Put away from thee a froward mouth, and perverse lips put far from thee."*—PROVERBS 4:24

> *"The mouth of a righteous man is a well of life..."*
> —PROVERBS 10:11

> *"A wholesome tongue is a tree of life..."*
> —PROVERBS 15:4

"A man hath joy by the answer of his mouth: and a word spoken in due season, how good is it!"
—PROVERBS 15:23

"Death and life are in the power of the tongue: and they that love it shall eat the fruit thereof."
—PROVERBS 18:21

"A word fitly spoken is like apples of gold in pictures of silver."—PROVERBS 25:11

Set aside some time today to sit down and write out the good qualities of your spouse. Think of all the things that you can praise! Think of words that you can use to encourage your spouse and communicate your love. It's a fuel that goes a long way to renew your relationship.

The Fuel of Quantity and Quality Time

Ralph and Janice were celebrating their fiftieth wedding anniversary, and Pastor Jones decided to take advantage of their longevity by using their story as a sermon illustration. So, he asked Ralph to come on stage and share some insight into how he managed to live with the same woman all those years.

Ralph turned to the congregation and said, "Well, I treated her with respect and spent money on her—but mostly I took her traveling on special occasions."

The pastor asked, "Where did you travel?"

Ralph answered, "Well, for our twenty-fifth anniversary, I took her to Beijing, China."

The crowd nodded and murmured in appreciation. When things quieted down, the pastor winked and said, "What a terrific example you are to husbands, Ralph. So, tell us where you're going now for your fiftieth anniversary?"

Ralph replied, "I'm going to go back and get her."

Obviously, this isn't the kind of quality and quantity time that fuels a relationship.

God teaches us in 1 Peter 3:7, "Likewise, ye husbands, dwell with them according to knowledge, giving honour unto the wife, as unto the weaker vessel...." The word *dwell* means to settle down and spend some time together. The phrase *according to knowledge* refers to the husband making every effort to know and understand the heart and desires of his wife.

Sometimes our marriages are literally on "the ragged edge" for one simple reason—we haven't spent time together. This is without a doubt, one of the most critical fuels that you can put onto the fire of your love. Time together is pivotal to keeping your love burning brightly!

We live in a busy day. In this technologically advanced age of information, there is a river of opportunities flowing our way—many are good and many are bad. So often we jump into the current of that river, trying to take in and partake in the entertainment, the trends, and the pleasures of secular society—and usually it's our personal relationships at home that suffer.

Instead of spending hours talking, visiting, and enjoying those we love; we sit for hours in front of a computer screen, a TV, a video game, or an inanimate interest.

I challenge you to date your spouse weekly. I challenge you to block off several days every six months to get away together—retreat and re-create your love and your commitment! Turn *off* the TV and the computer and turn *toward* each other!

Are you starving your marriage simply because you're giving your best time to other things? If so, the flames of your love will grow cold. Take a good look at your schedule, and deliberately schedule "fresh wood" for your fire. Intentionally plan, on a weekly basis, when you will give your spouse and your marriage relationship quantity and quality time.

God's first recorded thought on marriage is simply, "It is not good that the man should be alone; I will make him an help meet for him" (Genesis 2:18). God doesn't intend for your marriage to be two lives existing separately. Marriage is His cure for loneliness, but when we fail to renew that relationship on a regular basis, we end up "married but lonely"!

Renewing a relationship isn't difficult, but it is vital! It's as easy as fueling a fire. Love does not maintain itself and relationships are not static. How is your fire? Which direction is your relationship changing? Stop expecting your marriage to be self sustaining and start breathing fresh air into it!

Jump into the process of renewal and keep growing that fire on a daily and weekly basis!

A Faith Full Marriage

One husband was applying his position over his wife far too authoritatively, creating perpetual conflict in the marriage.

Finally, in an attempt to bring him "back down to earth" his wife shared some insight about her prayer life.

She said, "I've been praying for God to help us stop all of this arguing by taking one of us to Heaven. And when He answers my prayer, I'm moving in with my sister."

While that prayer may be an expression of faith, that's not exactly the kind of "Faith Full Marriage" that we've been trying to discover in these pages.

We've covered a lot of ground in this short book. We've seen that faith is monumental in our marriages! We've seen that faith is required to build a great marriage. We've seen that every marital challenge is usually the result of a paradox—a truth that doesn't seem true, until you apply it and act upon it in faith.

We've seen we must develop a "Faith Full Marriage" on three levels. We've seen the faith to commit, the faith to yield, and the faith to renew!

What a different marriage relationship these three steps of faith produce! In contrast to the 50% divorce rate of the twenty-first century, this marriage will be growing, vibrant, selfless, encouraging, and alive with love and strength.

Friend, God desires to give you a better marriage than you have ever imagined! Marriage is His idea, and it still works. In fact, He's your only hope. *Faith* is the *only* path to marriage the way it was designed!

May God bless you as you strive to commit by faith, yield by faith, and renew by faith!

As you set this book down, take a moment to bow before the Lord and ask Him to help you develop a marriage that is full of faith, growing in faith, and established upon the faith of Christ.

> *"Rooted and built up in him, and stablished in the faith, as ye have been taught, abounding therein with thanksgiving."*—COLOSSIANS 2:7

For additional copies of this minibook or for more information about other books and resources from Striving Together Publications,

✉	**WRITE**	Striving Together Publications 4020 E. Lancaster Blvd. Lancaster, CA 93535
☎	**CALL**	800.201.7748
⌨	**EMAIL**	info@strivingtogether.com
🖱	**GO ONLINE**	www.strivingtogether.com

About the Author

Paul Chappell is the senior pastor of Lancaster Baptist Church and the president of West Coast Baptist College in Lancaster, California. He is a dynamic preacher of the Word of God, an author, and a committed husband and father. He and his family love serving the Lord and spending time together.

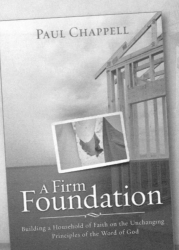

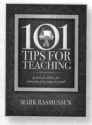

Visit us online

strivingtogether.com

dailyintheword.org

wcbc.edu

lancasterbaptist.org